The
Alien
Files

Paul McEvoy

CHELSEA HOUSE
PUBLISHERS
A Haights Cross Communications ✦ Company

This hard cover edition first published in 2005
by Chelsea House Publishers

CHELSEA HOUSE
P U B L I S H E R S
A Haights Cross Communications Company

Published by
Sundance Publishing
P.O. Box 740
One Beeman Road
Northborough, MA 01532–0740
800-343-8204
www.sundancepub.com

Copyright © text Paul McEvoy
Copyright © illustrations Luke Jurevicius,
Lloyd Foye, and Cliff Watt

First published 2002 by
Blake Education, Locked Bag 2022, Glebe 2037, Australia
Exclusive United States Distribution: Sundance Publishing

Design by Cliff Watt in association with
Sundance Publishing

The Alien Files
ISBN 0-7910-8431-0   CIP applied for

Photo Credits:
back cover (right): NASA; p. 6: (left) photolibrary.com; p. 6 (top): NASA;
p. 7: photolibrary.com; p. 11 (top): Mary Evans Picture Library; p. 12 (top):
Mary Evans Picture Library; p. 17 (bottom): The Kobal Collection/Columbia;
p. 18: Mary Evans Picture Library; p. 19: NASA; p. 21 (top): The Kobal
Collection/Columbia; p. 24: NASA; p. 25 (top and bottom): NASA;
p. 26: photolibrary.com

Table
of Contents

They're Out of This World!

Do you believe that aliens have landed on Earth?

Have you ever seen a small gray creature with large black eyes and a big head? If you have, you are not alone. Every year, people from countries all over the world report that they have seen aliens.

Many people say they have seen Unidentified Flying Objects (UFOs), which they believe are alien spaceships. Some people even describe how they were taken aboard the UFO, studied by the aliens, and then returned to their homes.

Alien Signs

For many hundreds of years, people have seen strange lights and objects in the sky that they haven't been able to explain. When people first reported Halley's Comet burning through the sky around 240 B.C., they wondered if this was a strange craft from beyond the stars.

HALLEY'S COMET appears approximately every 76 years.

IT'S EASY TO SEE how a cloud like this, with its smooth shape and bright orange or red color, can be mistaken for a UFO.

While some people look to the sky for signs of life beyond Earth, others look at mysterious things on land. On the Nazca Plain in Peru, there are straight lines that measure 60 kilometers (37 miles) in length. When these lines were first seen from the air, they looked like an airfield. Did aliens make the lines to guide their spaceships to land?

Look out below! Spaceships landing.

THESE NAZCA LINES look like a bird when seen from the air. They were made about 2,000 years ago, but no one knows why.

Spot the Alien

Does the idea of **extraterrestrial** (ET) visitors from another planet scare you? Or do you think it would be exciting to meet visitors from outer space? What would they look like?

Probably not very much like us. Alien worlds would no doubt be very different from Earth. They might have more or less of the elements that affect living things, such as water, light, or gravity. Just as we have adapted to conditions on our planet, an alien's appearance would reflect the conditions on its planet.

There is no proof that spaceships and aliens exist, but some people claim they have seen them. Stories of UFO and alien sightings are collected by people who call themselves **UFOlogists.** They study and follow these sightings as a hobby.

IF THERE WERE LIFE FORMS on the planet Jupiter, they'd find it hard to take a walk. Jupiter is a huge ball of swirling gases with no solid surface.

A Field Guide to Aliens

People have reported seeing several types of aliens. Here are some of them.

The Grays These are 1 meter (3 ft) tall, with gray skin, large domed heads, and black eyes. They have skinny arms. They are said to be the most common type of alien.

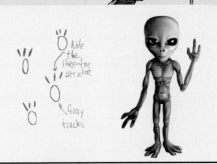

Chupacabras These are 1 meter (3 ft) tall with huge red eyes, fangs, long claws, and vampire wings.

Nordics These are **humanoids** with blond hair, fair skin, and blue eyes.

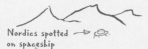

Is It a Bird? Is It a Plane?

When a new alien movie hits the big screen, reports of alien activity often increase. A new book on aliens can have the same effect. Many of these reported sightings happen at night or when the person is driving along a deserted road.

During World War II, many British and American pilots said they saw bright shining balls near their aircraft. They called them "foo fighters" after a comic that was popular then.

Between 1947 and 1969, the United States Air Force studied 12,618 UFO sightings in Project Blue Book. They discovered that only 701 of the sightings were really unidentified. The rest were explained as aircraft and satellites, weather balloons, the planets Venus or Jupiter, meteors, or unusual clouds. Some were also put down to very good imaginations!

THIS PHOTO of a Japanese fighter plane, taken in 1945, is said to show two "foo fighters" in the distance.

lien File 1

ate	November 30, 1989
ame	Linda Napolitano, homemaker
ocation	New York City, United States
he Claim	Linda Napolitano said that she was asleep in her 12th floor apartment when aliens came to visit her.

Linda said that she floated out of her apartment and up into the alien spaceship. There she says she was medically examined by the aliens, who then brought her home. At least three other people claimed they saw Linda being taken by the aliens.

Alien File 2

Date	November 5, 1975
Name	Travis Walton, logger
Location	Arizona, United States
The Claim	Travis Walton said that he saw a flying saucer hovering above the road.

Travis says he approached the saucer, but a blue-green beam of light knocked him backwards. Then he claims he was abducted by aliens. Five days later, he was returned—thin and unshaven. Doctors **hypnotized** him. Under hypnosis, Travis said he had seen short aliens with large heads and eyes.

Can You Believe What You See?

What should you do if you think you see a UFO? To get someone to believe you, hard **evidence** is needed. Try to take a photograph. Most people believe things they can see with their own eyes—although what you see is not always what you think it is.

CAPTAIN MANTELL was 25 when he died chasing what he thought was a UFO.

Thomas Mantell was a pilot in the United States Air Force. On a routine flight in 1948, he radioed his base to say that a strange "metallic" object was flying above him. He chased the object higher and higher, determined to find out what it was. But then he passed out. The plane crashed, and Mantell was killed. The official air force report said that he had probably been chasing the planet Venus.

Photo Fakes and Forgeries

How can you recognize a fake photograph?

DIFFERENCES IN TEXTURE OR GRAIN. A faked UFO has been **superimposed** on another image.

BLURRED IMAGES. The photographer has tried to hide exactly what the images are.

DIFFERENT LIGHT PATTERNS. Two or more photos have been superimposed.

Suspicions and Facts

Thousands of people all over the world have reported seeing aliens. Are they all wrong? Or is there some secret that the rest of us don't know...?

Many people believe aliens have already landed on Earth. They even think governments around the world are keeping alien visits a secret. For example, what happened in the small town of Roswell, New Mexico, in 1947? More than 50 years later, some people still think that the events in Roswell are very mysterious.

Crash Landing

One night in July 1947, there was a fierce thunderstorm near a small town in New Mexico called Roswell. The wind roared and lights seemed to explode in the sky. The next day, rancher William "Mac" Brazel rode out to check his sheep. What he discovered on his land puzzled him. Pieces of rubber, tinfoil, and tough paper were lying everywhere on the ground. Mac had heard rumors of strange flying discs that had been seen in the air during the last few days Had this material come from the flying discs?

Mac collected some of the material and took it home. He showed it to his neighbors, then he drove into town to give the material to the sheriff in Roswell. The sheriff turned the material over to the United States Air Force.

SOME PEOPLE BELIEVE that the strange wreckage Mac Brazel found on his ranch was a close encounter of the second kind—a CE2.

Q: What did the alien say to the Earthling?

A: #@$ %&^* (!@# # $^@ $@^ !

Types of Close Encounters (CEs)

UFOlogists describe five levels of close encounters (CEs), beginning with CE1.

CE1: Seeing a spacecraft.
CE2: Seeing some physical evidence of alien presence such as scorch marks or wreckage.
CE3: Seeing aliens.
CE4: Being **abducted,** or taken, by aliens.
CE5: Talking to aliens.

IN THE MOVIE *Close Encounters of the Third Kind* (1977), the characters saw aliens.

17

Fact or Fiction?

The United States Air Force studied the material from Roswell. The air force said that it came from a weather balloon that had crashed.

For many years, nothing further was said about Roswell. Then in 1978, a newspaper article said that the material found by Mac Brazel was actually wreckage from a UFO! It also said that the United States Air Force was trying to hide the truth.

AN OFFICER at Roswell Air Force Base shows the wreckage found by Mac Brazel.

Soon there were stories of eyewitnesses who had seen the air force carrying alien bodies away from the crash site. There were books and television shows about the "Roswell incident." It became the most talked about event in UFO circles. But what actually happened at Roswell? There is no evidence that a UFO crashed. But there is evidence that the material came from a weather balloon.

SCIENTISTS launch balloons like this one to collect information on temperature and wind. But to some people, they look like UFOs.

Aliens Among Us?

If aliens have landed at Roswell and other places on Earth, why don't we see them more often? Or do we . . .?

Some people think that aliens are living among us. They say that many of these aliens disguise themselves as Men in Black who warn people not to talk about their own alien encounters. Other people think that these Men in Black are special government agents who are trying to track down the aliens who are living among us.

There have been reports of Men in Black sightings from all over the world. But do they exist? Or do people read about them and see them in movies, then imagine that they have really seen them? We may never know.

Reporting UFOs

If you want to watch the skies and do a bit of UFO spotting yourself, be ready to write down the details.

- Event date
- Event time
- Weather conditions
- Number of witnesses
- Shape of craft
- Number of craft seen
- Full description

A GOVERNMENT AGENT, played by Will Smith, has a close encounter with an alien in the movie *Men in Black* (1997).

Alien File 3

Artist's view of
Man in Black

Date	September 1976
Name	Dr. Herbert Hopkins, UFOlogist
Location	Maine, United States
The Claim	Dr. Herbert Hopkins was investigating a UFO sighting in Maine when he said he had an unexpected visitor.

Dr. Hopkins claimed that his visitor was a man dressed in a black suit, hat, and tie. The visitor was totally bald, without any eyebrows or eyelashes. This strange man told Dr. Hopkins to stop investigating UFOs. Dr. Hopkins said he was so frightened that he did stop!

21

Calling All Aliens!

Space is BIG. Very BIG! But is this where we will find the evidence that aliens exist?

For many years, the search for other intelligent life in the universe has continued. Right now, unmanned space probes are leaving our solar system on a long journey, perhaps to strange, new worlds. Huge radio telescopes are searching for radio signals from the stars. If there is life out there in the endless, **infinite** universe, we want to find it!

It's Not Called Space for Nothing!

Our galaxy, the Milky Way, has billions of stars. With billions of galaxies in the universe, many scientists believe that alien life forms must exist somewhere out there. Our sun is a star that is about 150 million kilometers (93 million miles) away from us. The next closest star to Earth is 40 trillion kilometers (25 trillion miles) away.

If aliens are out there, they are a long way away from us! If you could explore outer space, you would need a very fast spaceship. A trip to the nearest star would take about 75,000 years. That's a very long time away from home.

THIS PICTURE of part of the universe was taken by the Hubble Space Telescope. It shows many of the different-shaped galaxies that make up the universe.

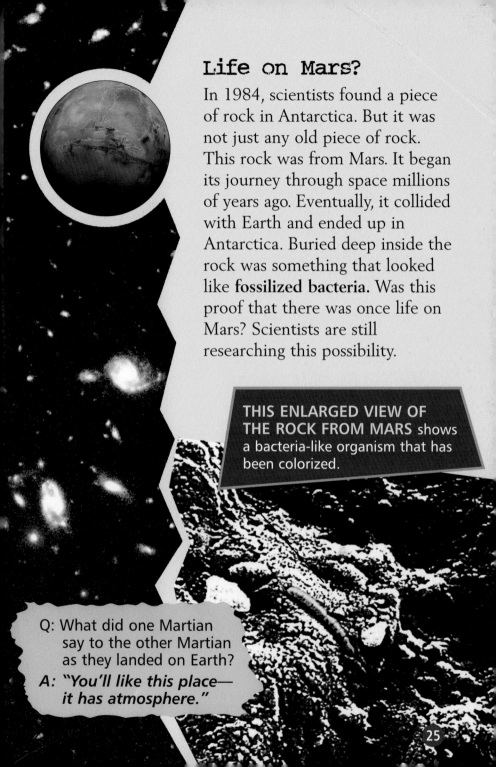

Life on Mars?

In 1984, scientists found a piece of rock in Antarctica. But it was not just any old piece of rock. This rock was from Mars. It began its journey through space millions of years ago. Eventually, it collided with Earth and ended up in Antarctica. Buried deep inside the rock was something that looked like **fossilized bacteria.** Was this proof that there was once life on Mars? Scientists are still researching this possibility.

THIS ENLARGED VIEW OF THE ROCK FROM MARS shows a bacteria-like organism that has been colorized.

Q: What did one Martian say to the other Martian as they landed on Earth?

A: *"You'll like this place— it has atmosphere."*

Life Beyond Earth

The fastest way to travel through space is at the speed of light. The **speed of light** is about 300 million meters per second (about 186,000 miles per second). Because radio waves can travel that fast, they may be a way to make contact with possible alien civilizations.

Scientists continue to study radio waves coming to Earth from outer space. They look for patterns that might be an alien language. Scientists hope that stars similar to our sun have orbiting planets, like Earth. But even at the speed of light, radio signals take more than four years to travel from Earth to Proxima Centauri, the nearest star to the sun. So the answer to a question would take more than another four years to return!

THE LARGEST RADIO TELESCOPE in the world i. the Arecibo Dish. It is 305 meters (1,000 ft) across an is built into a natural crater the mountains of Puerto Ri

Can Aliens Break Codes?

The Arecibo radio telescope beamed this complex coded message into space in 1974. If aliens ever do receive the message, they will have to decode it. Then it could take thousands of years for a reply to get back to us.

A Coded Space Message

Reading from right to left: the numbers 1 to 10

The atomic numbers of the basic elements necessary to life on Earth

Formulas for the chemical building blocks of DNA

Shows the DNA double helix

The population of Earth at the time of the message

A stick figure of a human

The Arecibo radio telescope

Our solar system—the third planet (Earth) is raised toward the human

Do you know what this all means?

Basically it says there are lots of yummy humans on Earth.

Probing Space

NASA has already sent unmanned space probes out into the universe. In 1972, *Pioneer 10* began its journey into space. *Pioneer 11* followed a year later. Each probe carries a gold plate with a message to any aliens who find it. The plate shows our position in the Milky Way galaxy and has drawings of a man and a woman.

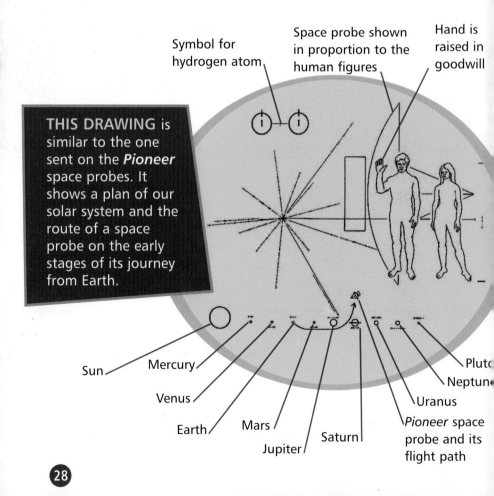

Symbol for hydrogen atom

Space probe shown in proportion to the human figures

Hand is raised in goodwill

THIS DRAWING is similar to the one sent on the *Pioneer* space probes. It shows a plan of our solar system and the route of a space probe on the early stages of its journey from Earth.

Sun

Mercury

Venus

Earth

Mars

Jupiter

Saturn

Uranus

Neptune

Pluto

Pioneer space probe and its flight path

VOYAGER 1 rocketed into the air in 1977. It is expected to last until 2015, when its power supplies will fail.

I'm an alien disguised as a planet.

The *Voyager 1* and *2* probes were both launched in 1977. They each carry a phonogram recording on a gold disc. The disc contains greetings in 50 languages and photos of people from around the world. The *Voyager* space probes are currently leaving our solar system.

Our message to any alien life forms is very clear:

We're still waiting for your answer!

Fact File

Crop circles are strange patterns of flattened crops. Some people say that they are caused by unusual weather. Others say that they are the outlines of alien spacecraft landing on Earth.

Stomp!

Stomp!

Stomp!

There are many UFO hot spots around the world, but Brazil in South America is the hottest. More UFO sightings are reported there than in any other country in the world!

Sometimes, the sky is filled with mysterious colored lights that seem to be "out of this world." In the northern hemisphere, these are called aurora borealis, or the northern lights. In the southern hemisphere, they are called aurora australis, or the Southern lights. They are caused by particles from the sun passing into Earth's magnetic field.

The *Viking* expedition to Mars in 1976 photographed a clump of rocks that looked like a face. UFOlogists claimed this was evidence of life on Mars. In 1988, when the rocks were photographed from a different angle, they looked just like . . . rocks.

This is not my best angle.

GLOSSARY

abducted taken somewhere against your will

bacteria these single cells exist individually or in clusters and are among the earliest forms of life that appeared on Earth billions of years ago

DNA the molecules that carry genetic characteristics

evidence proof that something exists or is true

extraterrestrial coming from outside Earth

fossilized preserved in the earth's crust as a trace of a plant or animal of long ago

humanoid something that is like a human, for example, a humanoid alien

hypnotized when someone is put into a trance-like sleep and asked to remember things that may lie buried in his or her mind

infinite more than can ever be measured; unlimited

speed of light about 300 million meters per second (about 186,000 miles per second)

superimposed when something is placed on top of something else, for example, a photo can be superimposed on another photo to create an image that is not real

UFOlogists people who collect and study reports about UFOs and aliens

INDEX